BONESHAKER

PITT POETRY SERIES

ED OCHESTER, EDITOR

BONESHAKER

JAN BEATTY

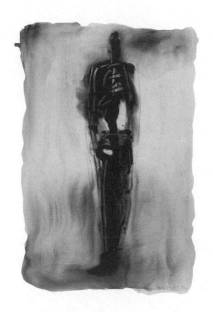

UNIVERSITY OF PITTSBURGH PRESS

The publication of this book is supported by a grant from
the Pennsylvania Council on the Arts

Published by the University of Pittsburgh Press, Pittsburgh, Pa. 15260

Manufactured in the United States of America

Printed on acid-free paper

10 9 8 7 6 5 4 3 2 1

ISBN: 0-8229-5779-5

for Don, always

In memory of
Big Jim Hollowood

What is the current that makes machinery, that makes it crackle,

what is the current that presents a long line and a necessary waist.

What is this current. What is the wind, what is it?

Gertrude Stein

CONTENTS

I

II

I · I LIKE REALITY.

IT TASTES OF BREAD.

JEAN ANOUILH

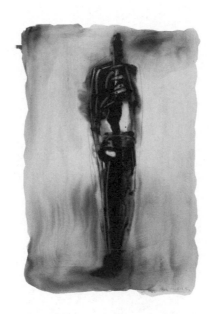

MACHINE SHOP OF LOVE

I like the way you play your guitar.
That's what I said the first time we met—
there's no explanation for being this corny—
just love or deception.
So,

                under the viaduct,
        under the old/railroad bridge of our ancestors/
        immigrant steelworkers/slaves of Carnegie/
        we rocked the back seat of a '69 Chevy/
        you pulled my chuck taylors/your jeans were long gone/
        goodbye to cotton/the rolling stones teeshirt/
        we're spinning in lust and oh
        steamy back windows and nothing
        can stop it/the rolling and tearing/
        machine shop of love, love—

its big plans/blue eyes/its you/
looking straight through the body/
in search of the heart/for two
weeks I waited until I proposed/
Let me think, you said/but no—

                the body,
it has its own light/own scent/
own can't-turn-your-back-on-it-glue/
I'll wait, I said, and did—

           for the touch
of your hair, the tender of hands/I love
the way you play your guitar/
compression/precision/the rock &
burn of it/the playing the/*yes,* you said—

PENITENTIARY

My name is Gale, you whisper.
I step back, you step forward.
I'm inches from your pasty skin, your
ice-blue eyes. *Where are you from?*
Philadelphia, I lie, in case you
remember, in case you ever get out.
You know I'm lying. You know my working-
class shoes, my cheap Lerner's dress,
my predictable blonde hair. You're 65/
I'm 23 in the old men's colony.

Warden says:
Don't worry, Gale never
speaks above a whisper to anyone.

I get to know you in the scan & rattle
of facts in your file:

> *4 years old beaten & molested/*
> *State Children's Home till 16/*
> *convicted at 18/sodomy of minor/*
> *victims 3–8 years/convicted/murder*
> *first degree/neighbor boy raped &*
> *strangled in bushes behind home*

The boy/in the bushes/his tiny body/
what/did you whisper/when you strapped/
his neck down?

The next time I see you/day after lockdown/
one of my clients/one of your friends/
raped & strangled/tangled in bedsheets/
belt cinched around his neck/in his cell/
Who do you think did it?
you ask as you walk up behind me.

I turn to see your eyes, everything
I'm afraid of: the salesman in the 5&10,
his misshapen head, eyes darting
like stray bullets; the old man downtown
who followed my Catholic girl uniform,
shoved his knee between my legs;
the man who put the ladder to my window &
masturbated on the brick/sperm on the mortar/
sperm on the mortar/

I don't want to help you/I don't want to
look/
                    knowing you were murdered/
                    as a small child/poor small boy with no heart/

          I'm looking for the name/of the first/
          person who hurt a child/

I was born with chances/were you born with none—
still I close my heart:

When I tell the warden
I don't want to help you/when I pull
my hair back/when I keep my eyes
down/when I quit my job/
when I see you again
& again in my dreams, a ghost
plays a white fiddle: all our sins
over & over in a thin whine.

MY MOTHER AND AUNT CHARLOTTE TALK DISASTERS
AT SCHMOTZER'S VILLAGE BAKERY

Did you read that when they found him,
he was missing both arms? My mother eyes the nut horns.

Isn't that awful, and he had a ten-year-old daughter
who identified the body, can you imagine?

My mother squeezes the sandwich buns, frowns.
I'll tell ya, if you don't get here before 10:00

on senior citizens' day, there's nothing left.
I know, said my Aunt, *Did you hear they found*

the black box for flight 800? She turns to the cashier
and says, *Are you all out of sliced egg bread?*

My mother heaves a sigh toward the sweet rolls:
Those kids saved for two years for that trip

with bingos, car washes. You never know when
you're gonna go. She orders some sticky buns.

Aunt Charlotte settles on the sliced white:
Mildred, they found his arms in a trash bag,

stuffed in a dumpster, can you imagine?
I knew they'd find them. A pair of arms.

You go outside to empty your trash and see arms.
I can't believe this, will you look at these

shelves? Now there's nothing left for us.

GOING DEEP FOR JESUS

> Run to the street light, make a right at the blue
> car, and go deep.
>
> *Sharan Watson*

1981, I'm on the back of a cherry
red Kawasaki with my boyfriend Stush,
my biker jacket bought with a tax return
from a year of waiting tables, stuffed
in my pocket the bad check I wrote
to see Stevie Ray play the Decade.
Down Beck's Run we hit Carson, my cheek
resting on Stush's firm shoulder till
the ground rises up with the hulk of J&L
across the river, steel house that burns it all,
an up-against-the-wall-fuck, thick &
ripping, everything is smokestacks
& yellow blaze. We ride the river roads,
looking for deserted two-lanes,
newspapers stuffed under our leather
for warmth. I want to forget my name—
everything but the sharp lean into
the next turn, the cheap slap of the wind.
Stush brags about his water-cooled,
two-stroke engine, but I just want
the contact high of leather, metal,
and the slow burn of a few joints.
Past the bridges & bridges, we ride
away from our fast-food jobs and
run-down apartment, toward the smell
of the Ohio, its perpetual mire, the rotting
docks and lean-tos, *to what we knew.*
I knew the muscles in his back & his
low voice would make me come
back to my self. We stop near the bog
of the river's edge to have hard sex

on the ground, our jeans still on,
trying to shotgun a moment, to split open
our lives in the brilliant light until
we *were* the mills, we *were* the fire.
It was then I decided god and orgasm
were the same thing, that if jesus
had an address, it would be a dark two-lane,
if god were here, she'd shove down
like a two-stroke in a rainstorm,
she'd let it fly.

KILLING CHATTY-CATHY

In the bare-bulb light I saw her pinkness, pulled her by the shoe from the bag of Christmas
presents under the stairs. What was she for? That fine, pink holding & squeezing, that fawning,
oh-so-precious? What I knew: you selfish, persnickety, you-only-think-of-yourself-girl.
Where was her mother? And where was mine? I knew her royal blue dress to be a bitter omen.
Her face: plump cheeks shoved up to her eyes, she was dead in the bag, cold under the stairs,
waiting for her child-owner, her guardian. Blonde-haired, blue-eyed demon: my Stepford, my
future: pull the string, *I love you,* pull the string, *I'm sorry/You're so pretty/* I pulled & pulled
the ring, trying to choke or confuse her. Her marble eyes open & open, her hair shining dead
through forty holes in her head. I strapped on my holster & pearl-handled guns, found my
cowboy boots. I grabbed Chatty, punched the rose of her face, put her blonde locks in a tub of
galvanized steel and poured in the water. She would be a drowning victim

&

I would live. The pink-pink skin floated for ten minutes, I took the body, wrapped it in a blanket,
stored her in my closet next to the buried dresses. Goodbye my vacant, my royal blue: You are
gone: smooth girl with dirt-streaked legs, dead, motherless girl like me. Now I won't become
the good, the plastic: pull-the-string-&-say-the-right-thing-girl of my adoption: years of no
mother surged inside me: a girl gets tired of a doll. The unremarkable cheeks, slow swivel of
the arms, the clicking, moveable parts, gleam of the black, black eye: there is no room for you,
blue girl, your black vinyl shoe that buckles into one hole: I could vanish into your ocean-blue
buttons, I could choke on the ruffle of your sock.

POETRY WORKSHOP
AT THE HOMELESS SHELTER

So I'm the white teacher reading
some Etheridge Knight poems to the four
residents who showed: *For Black Poets*
Who Think of Suicide—thinking
these guys have seen it all and want
something hard-core, when a black man
named Tyrone raises his hand:
These poems offend me.
They do? I say. *Yes, I was raised*
not to curse, and I don't see why
a poem has to use those words.

What poems do you like?
Langston Hughes.
Yeah, someone else says, *Jean Toomer, man.*
Tyrone says, *Let's talk about calculating a poem.*
Pardon me, I say—
You know, cipherin a poem—
Why don't you show me?
Tyrone draws this two-dimensional
image of this three-dimensional grid, based
on numerology, he says, in which each letter
of the alphabet corresponds to a number.

Look, it's like you start
with a 13, 25, then go to 8, 5, 1, 18, 20—
that's the start of my first line:
"My heart opens to the new world"—See?
I am stunned by it all—strange genius
or just strange? *How long*
have you been writing this way?
All my life, but nobody understands it,

I got boxes in my room filled with calculations,
I got plays and soap operas, and one day
I'll sell them.

I'm looking into Tyrone's eyes, beautiful
savant, wondering what to say:
I'm standing here in my new Levis and
Chuck Taylors, knowing I don't understand
either, and his desire humbles me.
Class is ending so I ask him to bring
more next week, but he has to see
his caseworker about his bad leg,
jammed up in a streetbeating in Philly.

Now I'm walking out of the shelter,
my white skin reminding me how wrong
I am most days, thinking about his sweet
numbers, his poems luminous with industry.
I'm opening the door to my car, counting
vowels: 13, 25, 8, 5, 1, 18, 20, my heart
stirring in the new world.

Aisle 6 at Giant Eagle, I slap
my bananas on the conveyor, a six-
pack of Ho-Ho's, three bottles of water,
and a *People* magazine with Tina Turner's
legs on the cover. I'm trying to be
anonymous, I glance at her name tag—
Marcy—she's staring into nowhere.
She calls to the checker in 7: *Shari, did ya*
see him? He's checkin out in 10 right now.
Oh yeah, Shari says, *I saw him.*
I have to ask, *Who are you talking about?*
Marcy says, *This hot guy, the one*
in the leather jacket, comes in every
Thursday, he's hot, go ahead and look.
I look over my shoulder: *Not bad—*
have you talked to him? Marcy twists
her face like I've been frozen for years:
I ain't talkin 'bout no talkin, as she
drags my Ho-Hos over the computer window,
never looking down. I say, *I knew that,*
but it's her I'm interested in—not him,
and I'm looking at her eyes looking at him—
she's got a look like the first time she tasted
chocolate—and now *I'm* gone too, wondering
if her lips are as soft as they look—
till Marcy says, *Here he comes!* and we are
forever bonded, me & the check-out girls,
in our head-down-sideways-glance
tracking his long, slow stride out
the automatic door—
Marcy, inches from me,
lets out the breath she's been holding,
Shari proclaims: *That is one hot man!*

and we're laughing, and Marcy is flushed
& resplendent and I don't want to
leave, I want more! More talk! More sex!
But I smile at her, say, *Hey,*
good luck, and I'm walking out thinking
about velocity on a hot night, a
thousand small heavens, my long
ride home.

MAKING BABY

Mother at the sink, spinning
her spatula, dead with no child. today,
a baby from the body of another. mother
salivates in her waiting. seventeen black-
birds build nests. she hates. their legions of
squawking babies litter her yard.
little fetus, little fish, she will be mother.
she bakes mincemeat pie, tearing
the bird from the lip of the world,
preparing the meat for the miracle birth:
she moves her dark hands over the body,
she cuts the neck, the muscle until
the trees sing: *blackbird*
& when the world opens the bird begins
to bleed: bloody mess bloody
mess to set before the queen: *thread*
of hair, animal head, white creamy fur;
suet from fat around the tiny
kidney; apple from the tree where
the song resides. she waves the cross
of jesus over it, lifts a piece
of fur to her, then curl of lip, she
bites down hard, calls it baby,
calls it mine.

CERTAIN THINGS

We were looking for kicks between
Pittsburgh and L.A.—rolling down
Will Rogers Turnpike in my '73
metallic blue Chevy Malibu—
when we heard "Kansas City" on the radio
and knew it was a sign. Bobbie and me
shot back up 69 to Kansas City—Kansas,
not Missouri—so we could sing
Goin to Kansas City . . . and mean it.
It was the song we wanted, not some
crazy little women, just drinking
and dancing, a way to forget
how scared we were. We ended up
at the Pink Corral with wild cowboys
who two-stepped us, swung us around
until my lucky mother-of-pearl flew
right off my finger and I knew that meant
it was time to go. Three days later
we hit Utah's saintly boulders and
salty hard ground where I learned
the true nature of Bobbie—she begged
the universe for a rest stop—no answer—
so we stopped by huge rocks and she said:
I can't pee outside. I shot a look at her
to see if this was real, and she had no clue
about how to, where to—right then I knew
it was over—I instructed: *Get up on a slant,*
one foot forward, one foot back, and
let it rip—make sure you leave room
for the pee to cut a path between your feet—
how did you get this far not knowing this?
This explained the over-reliance on friends,
the long, tearful phone calls—this was a woman
who hadn't yet felt her own soul

in the foothills of a desert—and liked it.
There's certain things you've got to know:
how to use jumper cables, drive a stick,
never fight with a drunk; you've got to speak
from your heart, walk with an attitude, know
the words to "Gimme Shelter"; change a tire on
a dark, rainy highway, say when you're wrong,
and slam down a shot; you've just got to know
how to look someone dead straight in the eye
and tell them to fuck off, stride across the room
and dance hard, want hard, throw down,
wear your jeans low and tight, you've got to
send long hot kisses until further notice, in short—
you've got to deliver—and you've got to pee outside.

MY FATHER TEACHES ME DESIRE

Once it starts you can't stop it:
My father leans into it like a hunchback
at the particle-board table in the light
of our kitchen, arranging his little world:
Vidalia with paring knife; Iron City next
to French's; open sardine tin/no plate.

His left hand grabs the onion/the right
slashes a fat slice/the right dips into
the briny swamp of sardine/lifts one
by the tail/down to the French's/then
plunges it headfirst into his cavernous mouth.

Crunch of Vidalia, then pump an Iron, and
we are livin now, baby, we are home—
me watching my Dad from the dining room,
the grunt and slosh of it all, thinking,
My god, he's eating the head—where
are its eyes?

What world is this? He's god and brute,
half quake/half precision, what kind of man
can stare down the milky eye of the sardine
sans flinch, then sever its head with
those same incisors he grew in his mother's belly?

Now he's starting again, reaching
for the onion, two-fisted and ravenous,
king of kings in this 6X6 tabernacle,
he's the holy spirit of torque and focus,
and this is more action than
I've ever seen in church.

I'm standing here at age 12, learning
that sweet seduction of revulsion/desire,

I'm learning real good that the guy I want
to marry is the one who can do the worst
thing without blinking, a man who eats life
raw, the heads of things—and what else
won't scare him?

Oh Father, oh terrible primate, I am one of you.
Together we can skin the rabbit, stuff
the apple in the pig's mouth, in this kitchen
there is so much I don't know yet:
That I can write this poem.
That I will want to die many times in this life.
That in ten years I will drive back to this house,
to this kitchen, looking for your glasses.
I'll drive back to you at the funeral home
and gently place them on your face
in the casket, with no flash
or fanfare, just the music
of my heart playing:
too soon,
too soon.

II • I LOVE THE BATTLE BETWEEN THE SKY AND THE GROUND.

JAY FLORY

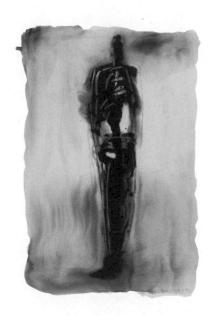

NEAR THE FOUNDLING HOME

1.

Mother of Blood, Mother of Skin, I don't know
whose life I'm in: Adopted's not chosen but plucked
from some womb/and still I'm the wren
on the porch looking in.

2.

Did anyone's heart have to break just to make me?
And which is the place that holds me to the ground?
I'm writing these lines, I'm shooting for the wild
heart of accident and still you have no face/
mother/it's 4:00 AM I'm rabid with my own
heart/empty & full with the shape of your face/
I'm starving, mother, in my no/story, speaking
to the no/one of you.

3.

Do you know the yellow scarf of grief, how it hangs
or saves you? It could come tonight/ten years
from now on any street: I walk in the still/born
night and there you are: air packed tight with
bone/hair/your hands first touching me/
I twirl to the huge zero of you, into all
your faces lining my dreams like barnacles/
now we're beyond the lump in the throat
to the shaking at night till my lover stops me—
nothing wrong—my bones shaking yesterday/
back to today, this time worse,
this time you:

4.

Mother of Blood feeding the tremor,
mother of rupture, bruise & shudder;
Phantom; Specter; Apparition;
Fracture & hoard; Quake & splinter.

5.

Just fill the "never" of looking like
anyone. Give me the story, broken & beautiful:
give me the body parts, detailed & sweet,
till there is nothing, nothing left faceless.

> Tonight I would say:
> *Tell me what the air felt like the last day*
> *you held me, the snatch of lilacs that*
> *brushed the dormer at the foundling home,*
> *how its sweetness hung thick in the air*
> *like a ticket out, all the hands, the boys'*
> *hands you'd lose yourself in those nights*
> *you'd sneak out, the magnolia talc and*
> *rosewater you'd smooth on your skin,*
> *trying to make one summer night*
> *last a year. How much you lost.*
> *When our skin finally touched,*
> *didn't you know you were home?*
> *Tell me: What happens to the body*
> *when you hand your child over—*
> *does it shake—or recoil into snake?*

6.

Mother of Blood, purging its young;
Mother of Skin, Guardian of Scars:
See Flush for atonement; see Purify
for evacuation, see Exile, Expel, see
free and clear.

7.

Tonight I'll tell you the lie of the story:

It was sky blue.
A sitting room with one rocking chair
and your hands, large and soft, cupping
my head of no hair. And every time you
whispered, your voice covered me
like a warm stream and no one else was
alive or dead. And when you whispered
goodbye, it sounded like every other word
and that warmth never happened again.
Then there was nothing, then nothing, and
nothing for a very long time.

DEAD JONES

I stall out at the Fish-Net Bar—no man
in my head—I mean the coke stops
working—and the dry-mouthed high, the
ricochet in my head eases to a slow slide,
so I stop the car and walk into the bar
with a moderate strut, you know the one I mean,
start looking for one hard shot or one
good man and can't find a trace of either,
so I take what's there. Did you ever do that?
Just settle for the second-hand, the man
who'll kiss you hard and ask for change
in the same breath, the minute man
with the jacked-up excuse for foreplay—
do you know what I mean?
Give me a shot of Ouzo, I say,
I like the way it makes the bartender squirm:
How can you drink that stuff?
I shoot it down, cultivate my strongest look
of disinterest, and watch the losers
roll my way, but I don't care who's
losing or winning, all I want is the
right-now-here-on-the-floor-slam-job,
the what-was-your-name-again-washout.
Trips to the men's room, trips
to the men's room, quick run to the Hill
with my dealer. Some guy, some car, he won't
take no/that's what I'm telling you:
this night/your body/your face-hurting/
jaw-clenching self: Look around and
you're not even up for a score,
in your dead-jones
rocked-out
life.

MY FATHER TEACHES ME TO DREAM

You want to know what work is?
I'll tell you what work is:
Work is work.
You get up. You get on the bus.
You don't look from side to side.
You keep your eyes straight ahead.
That way, nobody bothers you—see?
You get off the bus. You work all day.
You get back on the bus at night. Same thing.
You go to sleep. You get up.
You do the same thing again.
Nothing more. Nothing less.
There's no handouts in this life.
All this other stuff you're looking for—
it ain't there.
Work is work.

WHO'S THE PRESIDENT?

for Madison

That was the summer of slow-moving vehicles,
life was a steamroller, flattening thick tar
on a side road no one knew about.
My depression bloomed lurid,
a wet dream sticky with the ambivalence
of a dead end, reducing everything to one
pure blue thought—anti-depressants.

So I walked in with a hard jones
for the magic bullet that would make life
move again—still waiting for the get-off,
the knowing-it's-over-but-I-want-you-anyway—

At the deck, nurses white and name-plated
shuffled people like paper, and insurance
was the key word; the humped backs of
orderlies clustered by the transistor like
so much cream cheese—pasteurized and
listening to Bob Prince run down the Pirates and
Phillies on KDKA. In between innings:
Fill this out and have a seat over there.

The Bucs won, they shipped me to screening,
where I was double-teamed by interns
with clipboards: *How much do you drink/*
any trouble getting up in the morning/do you
work/what about drugs/are you married/live
alone/like your job/suicidal?/a student/
someone with you?

To which I responded:

I had two glasses of Chardonnay at a baby shower
last week (not <u>my</u> baby), and I don't know who

you hang out with (or if you live alone) but
most of my friends don't love getting up
and going to work every day.

This qualified me for the final cut:
the Sears Opticals shrink, stuffed
in a too-green suit, a mutant olive.
Who's the president? he said.
Pardon me? I said.
Who's the president?
Ford, I answered.
Uh-huh—and the year,
do you know what year it is?

1979, I said, checking his wiry beard,
pimento head, wondering about his place
in the food chain—
Do you know what city you're in? he said.
Wait, I said, *I'm here, I know I'm here—*
that's part of the problem.
How long have you had these feelings?
Look, I said, *All I want is a prescription*
for anti-depressants. Can you do that?
Do you have insurance? he asked.

Free-roving orderlies and rolling gurneys
glutted the hallway, the shrink in his underwater
voice mumbled: *series of tests . . . suppress*
certain impulses . . . a lot we don't know . . .
works on the brain . . . monitor your reactions . . .
Okay, I said, staring into the pinholes
of his black eyes, the jut and stilt of his jaw—
You're telling me this medication works
on the brain, you're not sure exactly how,
you want me to take it and see what happens?
Something like that, he said.

Doesn't that seem crazy to you? I asked.
Not at all—the steamroller lurched
in my head and suddenly it hit me:
The world can snap back your head into blue
before you can say your mother's name.
I ran to the cars outside on Bayard Street.
I was in Oakland. I remember it was sunny
in the United States that day. It was Pittsburgh.
It was May 19, 1979. The president
was in the White House.

MIKE'S HOAGIE HUT, MORGANTOWN,
WEST VIRGINIA, 1971

Yeah, I say, I want the job, it won't interfere
with classes, I need cash. First shift, 8–1,
400 lbs. of Mike stuffed into a dirty chef's suit—
he jerks his hand *howyadoin* from his backroom chair,
twelve-pack of Rock, leaning tower of porn—right,
it's not his fault—glandular spasm, psycho-trauma,
but the skin zines and a calzone dripping Italian
make me run to the grill and the short jock wanting
one hot sausage on the fly. Mike grunts, *Go ahead.*
It'll be a minute, I say, slap the sausage on the bun
while Mike reads *Big Babes with Hot Bustlines*—
this is *Wrestling Chicks on Parade, Confessions
of an Office Nympho, Tit-Fightin Amazons* and
Wedding Night for Three, Mike never looking up,
me and the sausage, thinking *What am I doing here?*
I'm a feminist for Christ's sake, marched with Jane Fonda
(pre-aerobic) against the war—now the tin of Mike's cans
hitting the floor, crinkle of skin shots, an occasional belch
until some drunk frat guy calls—ten hoagies, fifteen
minutes to quitting—I just cleaned the slicer and
he wants salami/well-done/hold the tomatoes—
I say to Mike, *I'll be right back*—
I walk into the cold night, to that crisp distance
of the academy, I never look back.

MODERN LOVE

Early evening, five minutes before
you're due home, I slam the dishes
in the dishwasher, squeeze rivers
of 409 onto the kitchen floor and
counters, smear it white with too many
paper towels, check the clock, listen
for the doorbell of your arriving—
Love, this is not my dreamscape,
my answer to romance's longing—but Love,
still I grab old food from the refrigerator
and sail it into the trash, call for
take-out with the breathy voice of
a woman in want—burritos again,
with enough jalapeño to make our eyes
water; Strange new world this shape
of our love: the details of our lives
stacked in piles of tabloids, month-
old pretzels in their lonely bag, and yes,
the paint peeling off the porch since spring,
no time now to wash the clothes. I do
the only thing a woman in love can:
clear papers off the bed with a wide sweep,
slide in the video, pour the soft drinks,
so we can eat in our element, our little city;
so we can tear open time to find the heart,
heart enough for us to fill our bellies and
fill our bodies with each other until
we surface to ourselves again, until we're
the only ones here tonight, and the look
in your eyes looking at me is the beautiful
sight, and my only complaints are two:
that I didn't make myself ready
for you sooner in life, that
I can't give better,
love you more.

LOUISE

Table 5,
single woman at a four-top,
smoking relentlessly.

Hi, how ya doin? I say.

Honey, let me tell you
exactly what I want—
Give me a cheeseburger with no cheese,
I want that medium-well, no blood, honey.

She grabs my arm, her smoke hits my face.

If there's blood on the plate,
I can't eat it, I'm sick to my stomach,
I just talked to my daughter,
do you have kids, honey?

No.

Don't ever do it—they'll break your heart.
And if there's blood on the bun,
I won't be able to eat, okay honey?
What kind of buns do you serve here?

I guess they're kaiser rolls.

Well, it doesn't matter, I know
what you have, I've eaten here before,
but honey, tell the chef to toast the bun,
not too dark—

She stares at me through thick glasses,
her eyes dark, magnified. She's maybe
fifty-five, her mouse-brown hair frizzed,
intractable. I don't know her losses;
I know her faded rose blouse and lumpy
wool skirt say: working class: apart.

And if you put lettuce and tomato on it,
don't put it on top of the bread.

I try to go back over this:
You said a cheeseburger with no cheese?

Yes, that's right, honey, no cheese.

So—you want a hamburger?

No, I want a cheeseburger with no cheese.

Okay. Toasted bun, not burnt,
lettuce and tomato on the side—

You can put it on the same plate, honey,
just watch the bun.

I deliberately loiter for a minute,
thinking people must often run from her.
She looks up at me like I'm wasting her time.

That's all, she says.

Now the fat man's being seated in my section—
the one who never wants anything green:
no pickles, no lettuce, and don't just separate
the lettuce and tomato—he wants nothing

that has ever *touched* green. At the door, the rich
saboteur who plants hair in his fries
to get a free lunch; the homeless young
mother who sips at her coffee
for hours.

Is what they need so little, so large?
I've walked into these strange lives
only to go back to the kitchen wondering
how to explain Louise to the cooks,
how I'll be able to get her
what she wants.

I'D GIVE ANYTHING

Survival's my only plan
when I walk into a Powell Street bar,
buy a piña colada, tilt my head fetchingly.
Ten bucks later the guy next to me
cruises my dream date, leans into
my body, says, *Honey, I saw him first,*
and I'm down to my last twenty.

       My Chevy
breaks down in the wrong end of the Mission.
Some low-riders give me a lift—I'm thinking
of pressure, hydraulics, what comes after
your last meal—so I call Allan, card-carrying
Communist cab driver from the Fillmore,
big brother of a friend back home.

I use the twenty to take him to dinner,
ask if I can stay with him till things
look up—being a communist, he says yes,
and I find myself in some strung-out flat,
a jar of mayonnaise and a bottle of soy
my only food, roaches darting at every turn.

       By week two,
Allan wants sex, and I'm lying there through it,
paying the only way I know how, wondering
what comes after broke, Allan inside me
collecting the rent.

Later I call the sister I hate, trying to cut
through the years to some kind of light.
She says I can't stay with her—I call
my friend Sherree back home, looking
for money. I'd give anything

for anything I need,
still I'm left hungry, hanging on the street,
staring at the black guys on the corner leaning
on their El Dorados, eating fried chicken,
until one of them says *Here, do you want some?*
and *Here, take this and get yourself*
something to drink.

I left my body on the floor of the city, in my birth-mother's crib, in the brilliance, the city of radiant mills—An orphan finds blood outside of the body—How could I not want that white-hot tearing? I lived for a year with mattress in car, twin bed in the back of a '69 Chevy/Great Cock of the Smokestack, Silver Warehouse of Dreams, are you there? I was jacked-against-the-physical/luminous with the drive of the almost hungry/how do you know where you start and end if it's not against a body in the dark? I was swirling inside with my drivetrain of anger/marooned in the world with a face and no name/am I here? I claim the dark map of my renegade city/I come from the monolith, the everything that still needs burning/I honor my dead who taught me the body raised up in work is the one true religion:

> *To the communion of saints/transmutation of sin/*
> *the lustrous, expansive surface of steel sheet/tattoo*
> *on the bicep/life with no back-up/the resurrection*
> *and the flight. To the raised hand/not the brutal silence/*
> *to home's burning ground in the body of the lover/*
> *to now & everlasting, amen. Give me the moment*
> *in fire/away from the awful knowing of the body/*
> *in the name of some father incinerate the nothing*
> *that is my birth/burn it all down & I'll rise up blood red/*
> *Let us pray to the hand job/the cock or the cunt/*
> *the lives of the saints & all their gleaming/I believe*
> *in the choice of the brick or the whip/give me the brick,*
> *because fuck you. Let it break/let it fall/don't*
> *talk me to death/dear holy ghost of the past:*
> *give me the light of a thousand rods burning/*
> *deliver me here/deliver me now/fire in the body*
> *of a woman in the brilliance.*

ARIA FOR THE BODY

1.

Baby girl on the lip of the world,

        readying.

Little one in the chalk walls of the mothershell.
No tiny star in the ribcage,
no hanging bird with no song.
Yolk of placenta, luminous ring;
Little girl architect invents her city:

              First the gill-slit—

              then the lungs—

in this terrible furnace,
this machinery roar, her heart's a ripple,
then a nudge—

        black seed for a sparrow's eye,
ganglia, sheaths—

        how to articulate the bone?

Here in the hothouse,
lips & fingers grow,
a wing covers her in the veiny blue trembling—

      One day,

         a swoon—

      fire in the body tunnel,
      roaring in the high air,
      a dagger of light,
         there's a war outside—

a thousand breaths push her out of the nest,

             the body

slides into new sky—
                                        the body
            in the new city.

                                    2.

There's the mother machine,
                            put baby on its breast—
nothing but a skinhouse, a bloody mess.

Little bird grown from seed to slippery fruit,
choking on baby-goo, motherblood, air—
Hands of the new city
                        cut the blue cord,
                        wipe the last blood,
                        blue moss of the hothouse—

                                            to the corona,
            to the new.

            Enough of you, motherglue—
                                Love, I'm here,
                                I've never been

so here so beautifully rapturously *I* and screaming:

what light
what light

III · THERE IS NO MOTHER'S BODY
IN A HALO OF LIGHT.
THERE IS NO MOTHER'S BODY.

PATRICE STAIGER

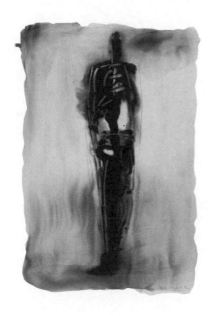

I CAN GET THAT ANYWHERE

Seventeen hours to think about nothing
In this too-drab hotbed of your departure,

This low-rent raw deal apartment that reeks
Of kielbasa, day-old burritos, and jism.

Why leave me with your Miles tapes, your Ramones poster,
That seedy silk kimono from the Village street fair?

Why today, when my Astrocalendar says it's Hendrix's
Birthday, and to watch out for heavy machinery?

It's just me and this refrigerator hum, the hiss
And wince of this jacked-up radiator, one drawerful

Of nite-lite condoms. Short-change artist.
Gas-and-run boy. Just two days ago I decided

The bridge of your nose looked almost regal,
Your too-sweet talk slid down the banister of my desire;

Don't think for a moment that your forearms weren't involved.
It's that crack of chemistry I wanted, those few blue

Crystal moments when my body stuns my mind into aaaahhhh.
But I can get that anywhere. Don't think

It's your fuck-me swagger, your London kick-boots,
Although I've never seen any quite like them.

MY FATHER TEACHES ME SOLIDARITY

My Dad wore his VFW hat in the house.
Every night he'd yell at the eleven o'clock news,
his local #5012 pin from the Elmer J. Zeiler Post
would bob at the brim: *They oughta hang the bastards!*
when the cops escorted some young criminal
from court to jail. He'd shake his fist
at the public defenders: *Do what they do
in them Arab countries—if you steal,
cut off your hand.*

I'd nod my head like I knew what propelled him.
I took sides. Not: my mother, cautious
in her rocker, directly under the carving
of Mary on the wall—the one shipped bulk
with the other maryheads from Rome to St. Gabriels.

She'd lift her head from the *Reader's Digest:*
*Bob, will you lower your voice? I've never seen
anything so ridiculous as you screaming at the TV.
Don't tell me,* he'd say. *For years I was a mealy-
mouthed kid. You see where it got me?
I'll say what I gotta say.*

Later, he'd sit in the dark of the back porch.
I'd watch from the kitchen as he swung
a longneck of Duquesne to his mouth,
then let out a husky exhale.
What secrets would such a man keep
between him and him?

Afraid he'd be alone in this afterworld,
I'd ask how he was doing, and he'd always
say the same thing: *Everything's copacetic,*
come out and sit with your old man.
Just him and the too-sweet candles in their netting
burning to keep the insects away: a lone yellow
bulb shone a ghost's light over the cast-iron railing.

AT BUCKEY'S, SHERIDAN, WYOMING

Girl in 5 said "Sorry, sir, I'm closed."
Whadya mean, closed?
I made it here from Clearmont in 15 minutes, and you're
tellin me you're closed?
"Sorry, sir, if you could just—"
If I could just, then I wouldn't be in this mess.
Look, I was a paratrooper in the war, man—
you wouldn't make it for a minute—talk about a rush—
I did two tours of duty in Vietnam—they said I was
paranoid-schizoid or some such thing—I just wanted
to go home, so I started killin everything—us, them,
animals, you—I didn't care.
I wanted to go home,
figured that'd get me home.
And it worked.
How do you kill day after day, then they tell you to stop?
Then you're supposed to come home "normal"?
The check-out girl was shaking, everybody
stopped.
I'll tell ya what:
I could rearrange this whole town in 24 hrs.—
just give me a backhoe overnight—
I'm tellin ya,
you wouldn't recognize a thing.

REPORT FROM THE SKINHOUSE

I went looking for the body.

The apple, tree, the river.
Gliding voice, curve of arm,
pearly blue uterus.

Muscled calf, the neptune green
eye, blood with the same
taste as mine.

Why do I write my report this way?
An adopted child needs to find a face.

What does a real mother's body look like?
River, chalkline, bloody cave?

I am replica of nothing.

birthmother, conjurer, boneshaker, witch,
let me smell your skin just once,
I'll give you your bloody daughter.

DRIVE, SHE SAID

Every day people are straying away from the church
and going back to God.

Lenny Bruce

Kissing was a crime against god—
unless there was no full frontal embrace,
no tongue, & duration of 5 seconds or less—
Sister Vincentia's burning descriptions
turned me on—all that body under her robes—
I wanted redemption, but not from her,
god's angel who body-slammed us
against the chalkboards.

I put her in a box. *Yes,* I said,
to Mike Augustine, to necking in the back
of the Hollywood Theatre, *yes* to his urging hands,
to being alive. I packed up my 10-year-old self,
the one who prayed for world peace as she blew
out her birthday candles. I still have her.

This is for the sexy Hare Krishna boy
at the "up" escalator in Kaufmann's,
his shimmering peach robe & landlocked hair
flowing brown from the back of his skull.
I wanted him. I wanted him to tell me what
drove him to dress up for god.

He explained the nature of illusion,
the material world wasn't real—I watched
his thick lips move into each new
delicious word until I was ready
for the group feasts. Sex, he said,
was decided by the Maharishi—*who* would
unite with *whom* & when & then I said no
to those lips, yes to the fourth floor,
Junior dresses & lingerie.

I've seen believers fall over for god
at the touch of a minister's hand—
Who's to say what *holy* is?
The blazing tabernacle? The black
vinyl American back seat, the cock/
the slit/the first clumsy groping?

BONESHAKER

Sometimes you just have to cut & run.

•

I was in the virgin court, sweet flower
at the feet of the May Queen—and
beating up boys in the playground, I was
a pitiful 35 on the shrink's GAF scale
(global assessment of functioning):
defiant at home/poor impulse control/
my wild girl fire was spinning—
they told me to shut up, be sweet, keep
your shirt on—I laced my black hi-tops,
loaded my cousin's shotgun.

•

Don't lose your place.

> *Stand in line to see*
> *the priest each day.* He hugs us
> too tight, too long.

> Mrs. Reid ties us to chairs,
> hits us with rulers
> for flirting with boys.

> The diocese says: *these*
> *are the movies good catholic girls should see.*

Say your prayers.

I learned the prayer of men hurting girls:

> *say hi to the nice man/be polite/*
> *forget the torn jeans open-road*

open-mouth-insert-cunt—any girl
who says cunt
is one.

When my old man neighbor
tried to kiss me,
I remembered my place, 15 years old,
it was second.

•

Did I say there's no place for a girl to live in this country of fear?

•

In the small place,
the fetus of the world's inside you growing:
clot of its bloody voice;
it's the size of a seed,—turning
your body against itself, cave
of uterus filling with blood of
world, world, baby fetus,
there, there.

You can never go back to your young girl fire, apple tree, fat spring air.

•

Girl in the wardrobe mirror.
Stares into the eyes of no one she knows.

Did you think you couldn't crumble?

You decide your breasts are repulsive.
There is no one as ugly as you.
You decide to break yourself.

Girl in the wardrobe mirror,
slams her arm against the door, forearm
hits the dark wood, Again, Again,

swinging the door on its hinge until
the body answers: *exquisite,*
until the yellow-green bruise and she is
home again in her body.

Blue girl, this is your new bruise.
This is your torn-jeans-open-road.
This will give you something no one
can take, something of your own
to watch over. Something to mother.

•

You keep cheap wine in your closet,
and valium for when your boyfriend comes.

He broke up with *you,* but every week
he picks you up & fucks you
in his car—in the backroad parking lot.
You pretend he loves you.

•

You turn towards him
in the backseat of his beat-up buick:
you see his mouth yawing & yawing &

no sound

the fat palm of his hand's
coming at you/shoving
your head down/*open your mouth*
his cock jams your mouth full/

again/again/you're back in the mirror/
you slam his cock to the back of your throat/
you don't care where your mouth is,

•

Now you got it, girl, you're starting to leave the body/
bathe in its sensation/drug it
so the pain stays dull/
where do you go?

In the space between
the hand clutching the car door & the floating off,
it's hard, isn't it, because it hurts too much, there was a man once
who scared you, there was a man a thousand times who scared you, ask
any woman,

She'll say: *He turned into someone else, he wouldn't stop, he grabbed me.*

•

When you leave the body, where do you go?

To a blue bruise/second grade/click of new shoes?
Apples/chiffon/the dead?

no
      you've got to

say that sliding

         goodbye to the body and go

•

Bitch, don't go crazy on me.

But you don't hear him, because the body,
your body in the backseat
is starting to break away,

and you see the body translucent(your body)
on the vinyl, legs splayed open and the body(your body)
full of water, so full you are a fish holding
an ocean inside,

you see your skin breaking apart, and there's
water everywhere, and blood, and the world's
in a sac on the floor,

you watch yourself pick it up, watch
as you bring it to your teeth, bite the sac open,
a thousand voices spill out onto the floor.

•

Floating

now

above your body, you see

so much water, washing the body,

washing the dead world,

you are

water
open mouth

sky

MY FATHER TEACHES ME LONGING

Empty eye of your onyx ring where
the diamond used to be; iron tack-hammer,
wooden cane, hat, hat—things I
dream on to conjure you back: thick
knuckles of your freckled hands, quick
laugh, Old Spice & Beeman's gum, your
life of work, work—everywhere, *love*—
over me, through, a wash of bloom, I'm
crossing Morewood, I'm the flood
of students, rolling buses, I pass
a tulip path and there you are:
Yellow tulip, singular, brutal fire,
is it here I find my foothold?
Pin of light that curses & saves.

RELENTLESS

In the beginning, when I asked you what sign
you were, you said *yield;* I was impressed—
most men, I think, would say *stop*
when making that joke—and all those brothers &
sisters you have—when I asked about birth order,
what position you were in the family, you said:
fullback; you save me you save me from my
flea-bitten self, my obsessive inquiring my
deep need to know, my therapist told me
to put on the raincoat of male oblivion
to stop my earnest, my motor-running quest—
so thanks for the coat for the walk down forbes
when we passed a young father with baby in arms
& the baby was cooing & you said to me:
why don't you do that?
why don't you just play with your feet?

THE WAITRESS ANGELS
SPEAK TO ME IN A VISION

Another tough Friday night, only fifty bucks
to show, I throw my stash of dirty bills on
the table, leave the change in the apron
that smells like two weeks of roadkill & smoke.
The mayonnaise stains gleam, otherworldly
in the beam of kitchen light. I'm tired
of waiting on drunks, coming home to myself
and these 4:00 AM flashbacks of men
trying to put their hands on me, regulars
who think they own me, I'm sitting here staring
at the cobwebs in the ceiling corner and that's
when they came to me: You've heard of
dust to dust, well this was dust to angels,
but these were real women with hard faces,
lifers in white, these were tough broads,
broads with cigarettes, pockets full of
guest checks and loose change—sassy babes
with big hair, gravelly laughs and downtown talk,
smackin each other on the back, saying,
"Honey, you're full o' shit," the whole time
my chest bursting with pride and relief
at the end of virginal blue, pressed palms,
and bowed heads. Death to Silent Acceptance!
No More Vale of Tears! Their hands on their
hips said: *Hey, we're brash, we're trashy,*
we're happenin—you got a problem with that?
These were no walking-behind-Jesus-babes,
no eyes-to-the-floor-floaters, these dolls
were sportin jewelry and mascara, they were
serious as a heart attack—and there I was,
ready to flee the corporeal glut of my life
for this hip heaven, when I asked to join them

and they shut me down: "Look, sweetie
this ain't no picnic here—we're on break right now—
flyin out to shake down some bad tippers—besides,
this celestial trip is overrated. Check it out,
your life ain't so bad."

DEAR MOTHER, MACHINE,

dear keeper, dear appliance,
      I went looking for your house today,

the mother-womb, for barren ones,
      where they make the ones like you.

I always knew your eyes were buttons,
the gleam not human, a patch/
crosshatch of light in the pupil,
A young girl could surely get lost in there/
never heard from again/never heard.

Machine shop of mothers,
      where bodies are made:

adoptive mothers are built,
      not born.

I saw the girders, industrial pulleys,
cables, grey dust, the hooks and the woodcrates.
I counted pieces of wood, bone & hair.
I saw the turning wheel, rivets, the steampipes,

this is a crime scene,
      torn page,

take photos. Load them in slowly, label them
bedlam, and where it says number, Count
all of them.

I went to the Steelhouse,
      the terrible city,

where barrens are made, What brilliance,
What genius, No organs, no heart,
This is the place of the bolt in the neck,
There's a mistake, those shark eyes all black—
she'll get a girl who can't talk back.

On Thursday, it's test day,
            a trial run for bodies,

the mothers go walking, dear mother machines:
armies of metal with long swinging arms.
This one's exquisite, her legs long and stalky,
spindly, weak—a fine pastiche
without any seams in gun-metal grey.

Pity the mothers
        who come out all wrong—

with rubbery hands & bloody insides,
a hint of a twinge, a beating pump?
Watch them rifle the trackbed for coarse-threaded bolts:
hunting a cork for their magical box,
                                    mad uterus,
they're useless and weeping, they're scalded in steam,
dropped in a sling to the subbasement wall/
        then boiled to a ball of scrap.

Here is the orphan child's truth:
Sometimes in sleep I hear the wheels grinding/I'm back
in the bone compound/terrible city.

Mother, you flag waver,
        best of the best,

no heart in the cavity, and bloodless—
        did you think you could make a real girl?

Tell me,
     mother,

why didn't your arm bend at the wrist line?
Ball & socket/toggle & hinge/hand me my ball-peen
& I'll make it new/I'll take a hammer to you,
mother.

     You dreamed of red babies
        suckling air,

you'd be a birther, a pod—it's not fair.
You got the fist, maternally clenched,
axle for knucklebone, I saw you there.
You're not the child I dreamed, you said,
Where can I drown you, leave you for dead?
I saw you hurt us, dear mother machine,

     your eyes were buttons,
        I got lost in there.

STEPPING OVER THE BODY

Stiff as a corpse/
down to the cement/a homeless guy with a cane
falls flat out in front of McDonald's as I step
out of Gus Miller's, I hear a little girl say:
Mommy, there's a man on the street—

then her elbow is snatched & steered away.
There is no rush of bodies, no frenzy of shoes,
hands, hair & jackets as people fumble:
only 5 turned heads, 2 women in business suits
who almost stop, 1 body on the sidewalk.

Then there are 2
medical students wearing those blue scrubs—
Thank God—then 1 of them steps over him
in mid-sentence with his colleague: just
raises his leg up & over the body & down
on the other side & there is no one.

No one saying: *Give him some room.*
No one: *Is there a pulse?*
Does anyone know him?
When I reach him/I prop him up/
see his dark black face/his wiry beard/
his clothes wet with piss & whiskey.

Are you okay?
Yeah. I steer him to the sidewall where
he can lean/*Can I get you some food?*
*Cheeseburger/fries/large coke/*he says.
What?
—Just a cheeseburger.

I get the food, give him a $20, he tries
to kiss me open-mouthed on the lips—*No,
no,* I say, and I leave him there on his
no-home street, thinking how easy it is:
the simple two-step over the body/
the leaning forward/careful

                         to let your shoulders fall
limp/avert your eyes/fold into
yourself like the valley of a scar/
then take any memory of this
and shove it/shove it down
hard.

The hard-boiled eggs.
    You said I was peeling them wrong.
    There was one correct way
        to strip shell from membrane.

    The dishwashing liquid. How I used
        too much of it. How I taped a dollar bill
          above the sink, called you a cheap
            son-of-a-bitch.

    When I put my fist through the plaster
        you called me insane. When I banged my head
        against the wall I wanted to feel
          something, anything that was mine.

Your scrapbook of body parts, all the women
    you fucked. You pulled it out for guests
    to review this one's cup-like breasts,
        that one's cunt—tight like a gift box.

    You called me *pig*. You called me *whore*.
    How I let you. You demanded sex
        one hour later, like a birthright. I'd pretend
        your hands weren't your hands.

    You accused me of cheating over and over.
        How I let you examine me like a doctor
        just to make sure I was *clean*.
          How I let you, that was the part.

Strip down, you said/I stripped to the hollow.
Two fingers inside me/you said
you could smell a man on me/
I left my body/

on the floor of the city/gone/
I was weightless/drifting/I was
happy to do it/

IV · THOUGH IT'S COLD AND
LONELY IN THE DEEP DARK NIGHT,
I CAN SEE PARADISE BY
THE DASHBOARD LIGHT.

MEAT LOAF

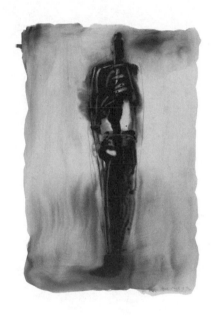

HEARING VOICES

Imagine you are a biochemical machine,
my shrink says. And then he says:
Blah blah/blah blah/blah blah/blah blah/blah blah
in perfect iambic pentameter. *You lost me*
after biochemical machine, I say.

          My first shrink wore dark glasses &
          had an Austrian accent: *You are quite*
          disturbed, she said. I told her
          I had trouble not looking her in the eye.

I like this new shrink, though. He tells me
his favorite movie is *A Clockwork Orange.*
I tell him he's sicker than I am. *Well,*
we don't enter this profession because
we are normal people, he says.

          But how do I tell him:
          There are 10,000 ball bearings
          lining my spine each morning,
          there are empty chambers inside me
          where nothing lives.

Afraid, I go for the joke:
There's nothing inside the core
of the world but the sound of a puncture
and a pile of Deepak Chopra's dirty socks.
Shrinks love to hear this.

          I want him to ask:
          What's the holiest thing you've ever seen?
          I want him to ask, but he can't,
          no one can dream the dream of our wanting.
          My father's hands, I'd say.

He can't stop the liquid switch/the veil
sliding down/fat pressing urges of the day/

> How can I tell him the silver
> hairs and freckles on my father's
> hands made me want to stay
> alive? Made me dream the old dream:

> *I want to see all the planets,*
> *the hot stars that weep dust,*
> *the haze that soothes them.*

I can't stop the/slit of blackness/strangulation/no answer/
no question/it's time/

> My father is dead.
> My father is here,
> the door to all dreaming:

> *I want to ride through large doorways,*
> *down the pale blue steps to the sea.*

HOW I FELL IN LOVE
IN PITTSBURGH

for Don

Maybe it was your blue eyes,
or that you gave me shoes
as a birthday present. Or maybe
when you showed me how
to cook kielbasa and pierogies
on the old turquoise stove
in my South Side apartment.
You started kissing me, pulling
me to the floor by the refrigerator,
making love under splashes
of grease. Maybe it was
your valiant reach up
to turn off the stove,
our crawl to the living room
where we woke at 5 AM
to what sounded like gunshot:
the exploding champagne bottles
in the freezer, all you had
so carefully prepared, breaking
into white, into all
that could never hold it.

WHITE EVERYTHING, NEW MEXICO

little girl anklets   this artpaper   my father's
handkerchiefs embossed RTB   virgins and legs
on a beach   new underwear   my mother's clothesline
supremacy and stiff laundered shirts;
fresh sheets   the light when you die   the new
tennis shoe   no one is one thing   gardenias any spring
pure cocaine   the pants before the bus ride   no answer.
paper blank paper   some dogs   some silence
this purity/your eyes/these clouds hanging
over Taos this day, white walls, large room,
space space space space

SPEAKING CORVETTE

Robert Plant moans through my bedroom door
into my mother's living room:

> *The way you squeeze my lemon, aahh,*
> *I'm gonna fall right outa bed . . .*

Zeppelin spins larger than the red & white record player,
I'm moaning face down in teenage angst, thinking, yeah,
I want to get laid, if it makes somebody say that,
                                           like that.

Next day I meet Pete's new cherry corvette,
'63 with a back T-roof. Pete the construction worker
with blue-blue eyes, bulging forearms and a nice set
                                    of car keys.

He's Italian, can't speak English,
but we both speak corvette—sleek rounded fins,
scalloped side cut-out/silver spinner hubcaps,

            closest thing to sex I know at 16—
I don't know *Italian* for wet between my legs,

but I feel it on the leather seats. Pete gives me
an American flag shirt and I wear it to bed,
rub the flag on my breasts
            —till the juice runs down my leg . . .

We speed over Pittsburgh on break from my cashier job—
hit Bigelow & sail to Polish Hill, crank down winding paths
to the Strip. I like the way people stare after us.

            Pete says,
                "Da shirt, da shirt, you like?"

I love it, I say. I want to lose my virginity
but am too stupid to know how—I stare at the dashboard,
How to say:

        red arrow to anywhere—in *Italian*?

I know the word in *adolescent* for get me outa here,
and *Pete* is it—I know the rumbling,
the jerking gear-change on a sidewinding turn,

    I know vibration is masturbation in *corvette,* beautiful,
    humming.

CROSSING OVER

You're the devil, my mother says to the blonde nurse—
when I get up there, I'll tell them to take you next.
If that's gonna make me go faster, I'll do it.

Mary mary mother of god meet me at the gate at the right hand of jesus,
meet me at the gate and follow me to the valley of kings,
in the name of god the father, amen.

                    Do you see him?

There's somebody's ugly face on the wall—
                    does it look like me?

I saw your face over on the window. By now they know about me
all over Pittsburgh, probably in Europe too.

When that light went on there, another goes out there—
                    Don't you believe me?

I can't die yet.
I have to clear my conscience.

                    You write about this. Make something out of it.

                    There she is, running across it—whatever "it" is.

Boy, old Clinton's golfing again. Hillary's gonna go her way,
Clinton's gonna go his. He's allowed to golf, isn't he?

                    Look at it, it's all chocolate—do you see the chocolate
                    dripping down the TV?

                    I see a woman's head! There's another, and another!

73

Do you know the virgin mary? my mother says to the candy striper—
Tell her I'm ready to go.

   I love you, I love you, I love you all.

There's a baby sitting on a table
   a woman with her arms outstretched
what is she saying?

We had clip-on hats we wore on our heads that said Xmas 2000,
you know, with an X? They had an accordion player—he was good, too.

   There's 2 little girls on the wall—
         and what about Glen Campbell? I don't think
         he left the building yet.

WHAT'S FOR DINNER?

How do you spell copulation?
with a "c" or a "k"?

    I don't know—look it up both ways.

Patty B. & me were looking up sex words in her father's huge Random House
instead of history homework.

Look at this— "intercourse: dealings or communications between persons or groups" —
useless—I want to know what really happens—are they talking about group sex?

    Look up copulation.

It says: "to engage in sexual intercourse"—this is rigged—they don't want you to know
what this is.

Why can't we just look up fucking?

Soon I was sleeping with a married man, took the trolley home for dinner. We had pork
chops and mashed potatoes. It was good. His cock was Mt. Vesuvius, we studied that in 6th grade,
the biggest thing I've seen before or since, we couldn't get it in.

My mother sat me down to explain the "Marriage Act" after I'd been fucking my boyfriend for a
year. I just nodded, said *Is that it?*

When I told my mother I was joining a women's therapy group
her response was American Contemporary, to complement the living room:
do you want peas for dinner?

    She said:

        Do you want peas

        for dinner?

I don't give a fuck about dinner—

the look-what-I-made-for-you-don't-you-appreciate-it/sweet preparation/what's on sale
conversations about this meal or that between friends, spouses, lovers, relatives, chefs on tv/
the pickled eye of domesticity in the 21st century/nothing's changed/shoot me now, don't wait
conversations—

      but yes, I want.

yes, very much, I've been wanting to fuck someone since I was born—I mean I really want to
fuck somebody, slam him in and jack off with him inside, I mean I want to bang his brains out,
rock him into the headboard, or better than that, the wall, I don't have a headboard,
I want someone's arms around me, doesn't matter if it's real—peas or potatoes, this body or that
body, I don't care—you can say inane things to me about food, as long as I get to fuck
somebody, are you getting this?

Let me say it another way:
I'll give you wads of money to never ask me what I want for dinner ever again.
I'll pull the skin up over my face and down the back of my skull if you ask me what I feel like
eating tonight—

      can we just eat it?

       How are you?

First day of the rest of your wretched life, does anyone really care?
I mean, how many meals do we eat in a lifetime?

        I think we should talk about fucking instead—

Would you like to fuck now or after the news?

And what do *you* want?

      the quick slam/
          bag-over-the-head fuck?

Or do you want the body—

face miraculous with lines & questions,
the whole beautiful, bags & hanging jaw,

the raging in & in
to find where we start & end.

AFTER THERAPY, I DREAM OF KEITH RICHARDS & THE FAILURE OF LANGUAGE

2 AM when I rolled downstairs
for water and aspirin and there he was—
leaning on the door of the open Frigidaire.
No heroin in there, I thought, and
I thought of hangover, every bad acid
trip I've ever taken—but no—
this was really Keith with his peach
scarf draping his neck, his black
shark-eyes, his sleek, defined telecaster
arms, and I thought of my friend Rhoda,
who loves to eat pickled herring late
at night and should I call, invite
her over? No way, I thought, I've got
first dibs. It was then I heard
the voice of god, speaking in clichés:
Honey, it's time to trade in the old
Plymouth and buy that red Mustang,
it's now or never. I thought of
my dead dog Dusty, how he chewed
the electrical cord in our living room
like so much licorice and lost a piece
of his tongue. How I held him in
my child arms and became him, the one
who couldn't speak—and yeah, so what,
I projected my precious longing
onto this tongueless mutt—So I said
to Keith, *Hey man, what's happenin?*
(I know it's weak, but till you've seen
Keith Richards drinking Tropicana
in your kitchen, don't talk to me about
language) He wanted *Mad Dog*—I wanted
to do him on the floor—then I thought of

my high school English teacher, Mrs. Smith,
who said: *Always refer to your notecards.*
But she failed me for unladylike behavior—
so I said hello to that blue moment,
I said, *If I told you you had a hot body,*
would you hold it against me?
I said, *I'll get the Mad Dog, let's blow*
this place—you first.

MY FATHER TEACHES ME LIGHT

7 AM I get the call you have died.
To get to the hospital before my mother &
sister & their arsenal of sorrows:
I rush to your bedside, nothing
has ever been this important.
I'm standing in the shaft of morning,
the light through the window splitting
the room in half: the dead body of you/
the living me. I talk to the air, tell you
it will be alright, look to the ceiling
for floating bodies: there is no you there.
The part of me in your heart, where is it?
And what is the body now, old empty house?
You said you'd come to haunt me,
pound your cane on the floorboards,
I'd hear you say, *Pay your bills!*
I hang your cane on my bedroom door,
I wear your VFW jacket & sometimes
old men stop me to make sure I'm not
mocking the War. I want to tell them: You
were the one who spun me into the fire
of myself; I am the one you left behind,
the one you saved while you were here.

ZEN OF TIPPING

My friend Lou
used to walk up to strangers
and tip them—no, really—
he'd cruise the South Side,
pick out the businessman on his way
to lunch, the slacker hanging
by the Beehive, the young girl
walking her dog, and he'd go up,
pull out a dollar and say,
Here's a tip for you.
I think you're doing a really
good job today. Then Lou would
walk away as the tippee stood
in mystified silence. Sometimes
he would cut it short with,
Keep up the fine work.
People thought Lou was weird,
but he wasn't. He didn't have much,
worked as a waiter. I don't know
why he did it. But I know it wasn't
about the magnanimous gesture,
an easy way to feel important,
it wasn't interrupting the impenetrable
edge of the individual—you'd
have to ask Lou—maybe it was
about being awake, hand-to-hand
sweetness, a chain of kindnesses,
or fun—the tenderness
we forget in each other.

My father could be a bird today, he is
so light. His radiation-bald head, his
body of bone and elastic skin, he's
standing in the examining room,
holding up an old ivory letter opener
in a carved wooden case. *Look! Look!* he says,
trying to tell his Japanese doctor something
about World War II. I know it's about his buddy
dying in a ditch & handing him this souvenir
from an enemy kill—but my father can't
make the words. He sways as he waves the ivory
blade, saying *Here! Here!* while cancer roams
his brain but we don't know it yet on this
windy October day. My father's gesture: a wish
to talk man to man: *I fought in the war. I killed
a man. This is my offering.* The puzzled doctor
looks over at me—

                but I'm lost
in the hall of a man's dark apartment—
he shows me the pearl-handled knife.
Do you like it? he says in a bourbon-laced voice.
My body says run, but he's big/between me
and the door/so *Yes,* I say as he rolls
the knife over the meat of his hand, traces
the blade like a body part he's known
forever, saying, *Isn't it beautiful?*
I know he killed a man once, stuffed
the body in the trunk, still alive, I know
he used to fuck me different, hand around
my neck like jail, mattress on the floor,
I say, *We're friends, aren't we?* and he
smiles, says *Wouldn't you like to cut me?*
I walk towards his body, he lets me leave,
I want to believe in the kind beating

heart—that we each have a kill inside us/
a war we're fighting/what would it take for you
to let it out?

   —my father's still holding the ivory
knife, he's leaning & weaving, I catch
his thin body and guide him to the chair. *He's
trying to tell you something,* I say to the doctor,
He wants to reach you.

SEIZURE

The day the world turned inside
out, your teeth were snapping at
the dirty hospital air, your head
rotating in the cave of its own
world, waking the animal that our bodies
finally remember to be, until it cracks
the surface of now, spitting its animal
hiss:
      It's my turn to speak before you
go—and now *it's* out and *we're* in
the grab and brag of: *seize, seize,*
impulse haywire/please don't die
& what have you done
with my father?

The great doctor orders the family
out: *Please step into the corridor*
for a moment. The lone person is wild-
eyed and fighting. He is bashing against
the walls of the next world. I'm
crying in this ordinary hospital with
the walls still standing. They don't
want the family to see—

      My father, my ally, the strangers
are putting their hands on you, and I
am away, away in the hallway, and where
is the love that can stop all of this?

I sit by your bed and read aloud:
Zen and the Art of Motorcycle Maintenance,
a book I loved twenty years ago.
I'm pulling out all the old wishes:

Forget the shield of cars & windows,
let us be *in* this life, if only on the way out.

 Father, I'm reading for the star
in the story to guide you home,
sweet, stupid girl, I'm reading a story
to hold us both to the ground.

CRUISING THE BLUE BELT

Driving 51 North to Pittsburgh,
I saw the graffiti chalked on the underpass:

Things to do:
1. Kill Satan
2. Free Larouche
3. Buy milk

At last! I thought,
someone who thinks like me!
No, it's not that I want
to kill Satan or free Larouche,
it's that list—the things
we want to do each day,
how do you make it?

When you stop and realize
that even Satan-killers
need to think about milk,
it really takes you back.

And what *should* my list be
on an average day in this aching world:

1. Kill Rush Limbaugh
2. Find a cure for AIDS
3. Buy chocolate

Sounds just as stupid as the Larouche thing
—that's my point—
Like when I was driving home
after teaching a class on meter
in poetry, and feeling pretty good
about it, too—Terry Gross
had to come on *Fresh Air* and talk

about gangs in L.A.—and my list
for the day, which had been:

1. Prepare for class
2. Go work out
3. Meet Carole at Ali Baba's

—my list became silly, shallow—
and why was I on the planet anyway,
and what was my *real* list?

Like the time I met my husband
for lunch downtown, and, you know,
we were in the mood for Italian, something
with fresh basil and garlic, as we walked
past the YMCA on the way to Oxford Center,
there was a woman and her child wrapped
in dirty pink blankets, lying smack
against the wall with mounds of brown
paper bags around them, and what was I
thinking about—

Your list? None of
my business—but I'm asking.
Have you found a way
to walk around the world, have you
found a way to negotiate the pain? And
where do you hold it, the pain, and please,
if you find that list, scratch it
on the underpass next to Satan, and
leave your name, please,
leave your name.

NOTES

"Killing Chatty-Cathy" makes use of a phrase from *Blacks* by Gwendolyn Brooks.

"Poetry Workshop at the Homeless Shelter" is dedicated to the residents of Wood Street Commons.

"Near the Foundling Home" refers to Roselia Foundling Home, a home for unwed mothers in the Hill District of Pittsburgh.

"My Father Teaches Me to Dream" is in the voice of R. T. Beatty.

"Aria for the Body" makes use of a few phrases from the following: *In the Country of Hearts*, by John Stone; *The Walls Do Not Fall*, by H.D.; *Collected Poems*, by Anne Sexton.

"Relentless" is dedicated to Rhoda Mills Sommer.

"The Waitress Angels Speak to Me in a Vision" is dedicated to all the lifers.

"Hearing Voices" is dedicated to Dr. G.

"Cruising the Blue Belt" is for the beautiful world.

ACKNOWLEDGMENTS

The author and publisher wish to acknowledge the following publications in which some of these poems first appeared: *Cimarron Review* ("Cruising the Blue Belt"); *Controlled Burn* ("After Therapy, I Dream of Keith Richards & the Failure of Language," "Certain Things," "Dead Jones"); *Crab Orchard Review* ("Going Deep for Jesus"); *5 AM* ("How I Fell in Love in Pittsburgh," "I Can Get That Anywhere," "My Mother and Aunt Charlotte Talk Disasters at Schmotzer's Village Bakery," "Who's the President?"); *Gulf Stream* ("Relentless"); *Heart* ("Poetry Workshop at the Homeless Shelter"); *Indiana Review* ("Hearing Voices"); *The Journal* ("White Everything, New Mexico"); *Pearl* ("Seizure"); *Pittsburgh Post-Gazette* ("Modern Love"); *Poet Lore* ("Zen of Tipping"); *Red Brick Review* ("I'd Give Anything"); *Rickshaw* ("Cruising with the Check-out Girls"); *Witness* ("The Kill," "Mike's Hoagie Hut, Morgantown, West Virginia, 1971," "My Father Teaches Me to Dream," "Penitentiary," "The Waitress Angels Speak to Me in a Vision").

I would like to express my appreciation to the Pennsylvania Council on the Arts; the Pittsburgh Cultural Trust and the Howard Heinz Endowment and Laurel Foundation; Ucross Foundation, Clearmont, Wyoming; Hedgebrook, Whidbey Island, Washington; and Leighton Studios, Banff, Alberta, Canada, for fellowships and support which helped me to write these poems. I would also like to thank Marcus Cafagña, Toi Derricotte, Patricia Dobler, Gwen Ebert, Lynn Emanuel, Laurie Graham, Julia Kasdorf, Nancy Koerbel, Nancy Krygowski, Jane McCreery, Sharon McDermott, Leslie Mcilroy, Betsy Sholl, Justin Vicari, and Lois Williams for helpful comments on these poems; special thanks to Maggie Anderson for extraordinary guidance; Aaron Smith for extreme poem support; Judith Vollmer for vision & kindness above & beyond in shaping this manuscript; Ed Ochester for much-needed wisdom and generosity; R. T. Beatty and Big Jim Hollowood; Natalie Goldberg, Barry Lopez, and Barbara Zaring for their inspiration; Jay Flory for his big heart & unwavering desire; Pat Bernarding, bloodsister; Terry Miller and Moe Coleman of the Institute of Politics for kind help; Michael Wurster, poetry hero; remembering Sharon Shelton and Joe Kirby; Daniel Anderson for his fierce poems; Romaine Horowitz for her guts; all the girls, especially Sherree, Mary Jeanne, Niki, Stephanie, Sherree, Megan, Special K, and Kathy; the Madwomen in the Attic for their courage; Charlotte Thoma for absolute kindness; Bonnie Boone for showing up; Vera Hollowood, food advisor; Gary Hollowood, car expert; Bill & Jean Hollowood for travel support; Dan Morrow for mustard assistance; Lynnette Seward for kind support; Bounce for his sense of invention; Michael Lotenero for his wonderful paintings; Joel Grimes for true grit & beautiful spirit; Brad Coffield for his good nature; John Belch, techno-guru, for sweetness & funny jokes; Ellen Placey Wadey for teaching lessons; Rosie & friends at WYEP; Jodi Peppel & Susan Wind for burning obedience; Susan Smalley for inside information; Tamara DiPalma (COG) for trials of patience; Dr. G. for great insight and compassion; Nan for bravery; Carole Coffee for years of hanging out; Megan Chambers for asking questions; Joyce Connors for intense kindness; Madison (Mad Dog) Brooks for her relentless self; Rhoda Mills Sommer, visionary; and Don Hollowood, the one who matters most.

Jan Beatty is the author of *Mad River,* winner of the 1994
Agnes Lynch Starrett Prize from University of Pittsburgh
Press, and the chapbook *Ravenous,* which won the 1995
State Street Chapbook Prize. Her poetry has appeared in
Indiana Review, Witness, The Journal, and *Crab Orchard
Review,* and in anthologies published by the University of
Illinois Press, Kent State University Press, and the Univer-
sity of Iowa Press. Beatty hosts and produces *Prosody,* a
public radio show on NPR affiliate WYEP-FM featuring
the work of national writers.